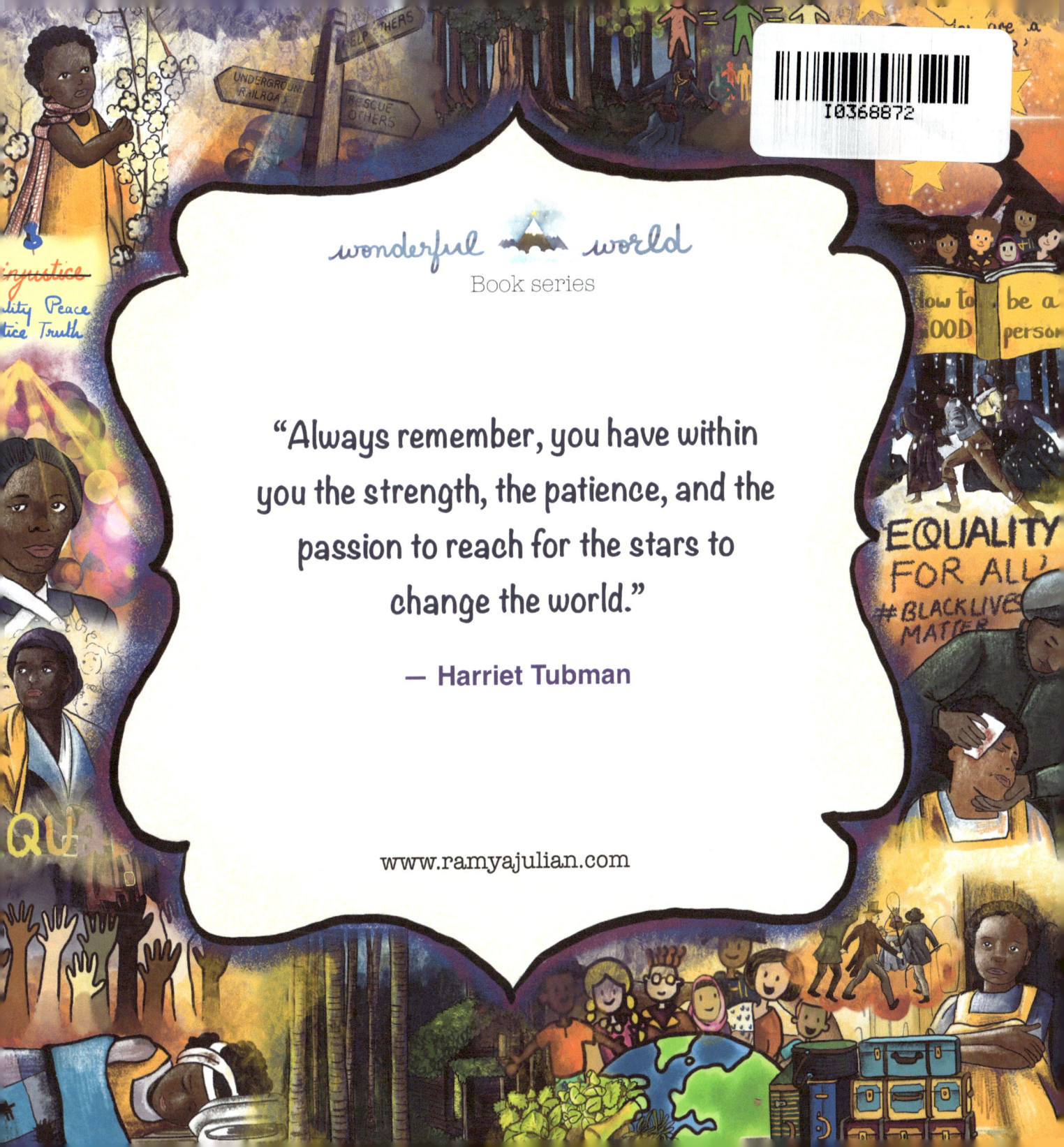

wonderful world
Book series

"Always remember, you have within you the strength, the patience, and the passion to reach for the stars to change the world."

— Harriet Tubman

www.ramyajulian.com

Born enslaved and forced to work all day,

Enslaved: Forced to be a slave
Slave: A person who is forced to work for someone else, usually without being paid for it. They are not allowed to refuse (say no to) work, no matter how ill or tired they are.

Harriet Tubman was given little food and no pay.

As a child, she was hit on her head,

and left to recover alone in a shed.

Recover: To get better after feeling unwell due to an illness or injury.

Though in pain, she began seeing visions,

Visions: Ideas or dreams

which helped her understand her life's mission.

Mission: A job or task that is special to each person.
(Harriet felt her mission was rescuing other people who had been enslaved.)

When she grew up, she escaped slavery,

With the **Underground Railroad's** help and her own bravery.

Underground Railroad: A group of people who were against slavery. They helped those escaping from slavery by protecting them, giving them a place to stay, sharing food, and guiding them safely to places where slavery was banned (not allowed).

She went back for the others, despite the danger,

Risks/ Danger: The chance that something bad might happen.

She wanted to help everyone — whether friend or stranger.

The worse the weather,
the more people she saved,

as they could hide better during the storms they braved.

Harriet did these rescues for over eight years,

Despite all the risks and her very real fears.

Risks/ Danger: The chance that something bad might happen.

Because being brave doesn't mean you're not scared

It means you use your fears
to be more prepared,

To face whatever happens,
no matter what,

And you're willing to use everything you've got.

Harriet was brave, kind, and courageous too,

A wonderful person —
just like you!

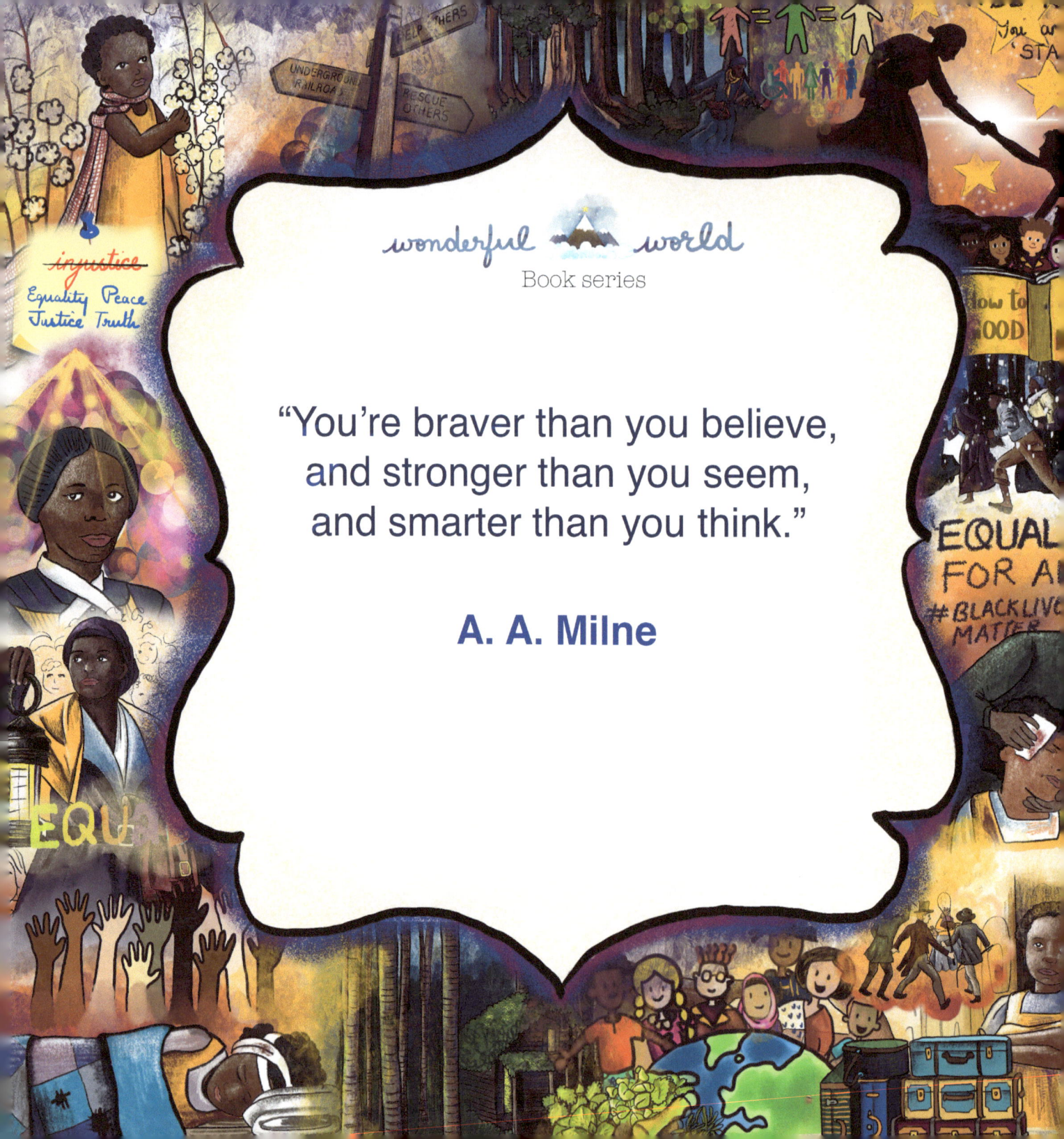

wonderful world
Book series

"You're braver than you believe, and stronger than you seem, and smarter than you think."

A. A. Milne

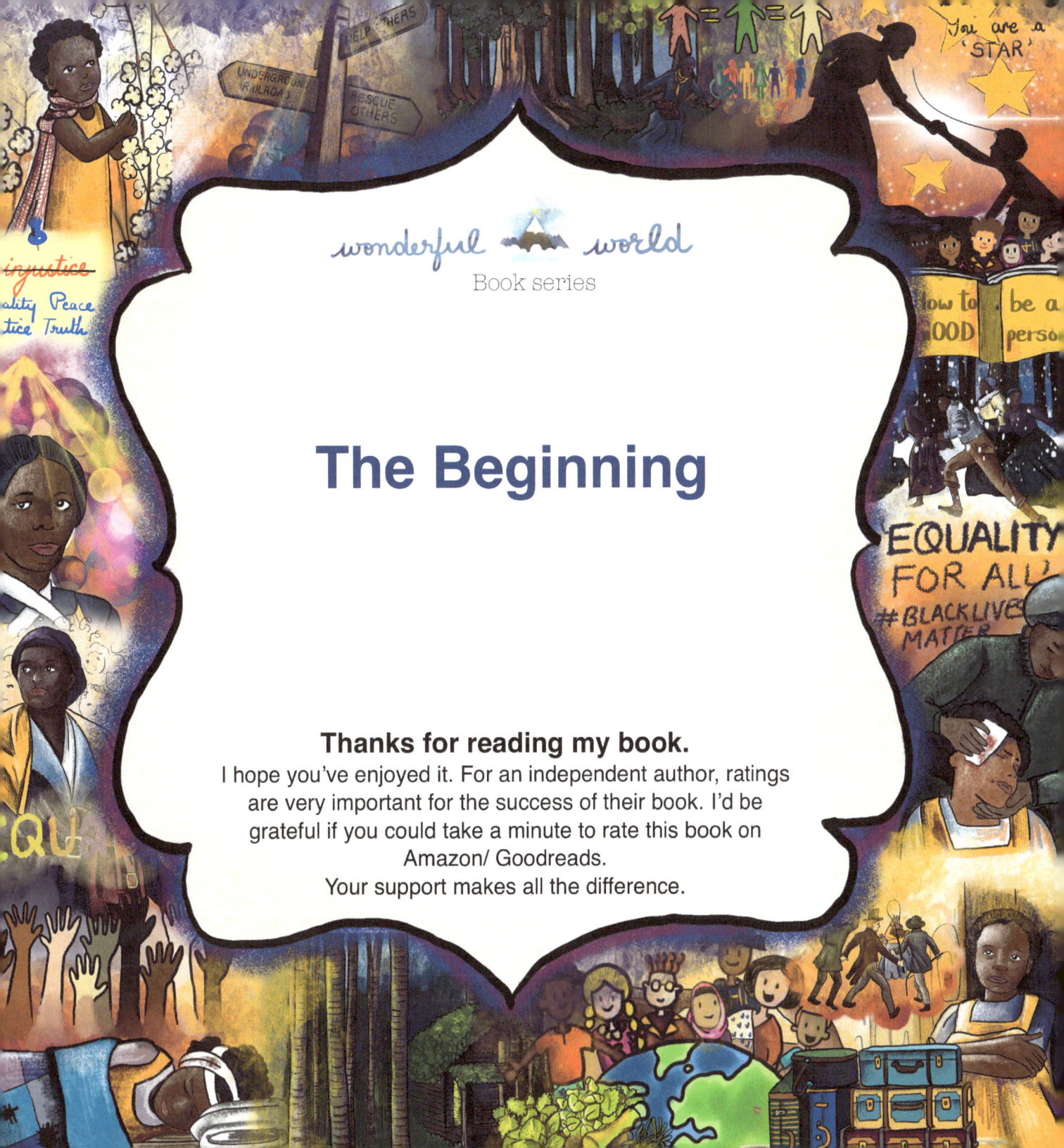

wonderful world
Book series

The Beginning

Thanks for reading my book.
I hope you've enjoyed it. For an independent author, ratings are very important for the success of their book. I'd be grateful if you could take a minute to rate this book on Amazon/ Goodreads.
Your support makes all the difference.

Glossary

Enslaved:
Forced to be a slave

Slave:
A person who is forced to work for someone else, usually without being paid for it. They are not allowed to refuse (say no to) work, no matter how ill or tired they are. They were treated very badly and with great cruelty (meanness).

Recover:
To get better after feeling unwell due to an illness or injury.

Visions:
Ideas or dreams

Glossary

Mission:
A job or task that is special to each person. (Harriet felt her mission was rescuing other people who had been enslaved.)

Underground Railroad:
A group of people who were against slavery. They helped those escaping from slavery by protecting them, giving them a place to stay, sharing food, and guiding them safely to places where slavery was banned (not allowed).

Risks/ Danger:
The chance that something bad might happen.

HARRIET TUBMAN

Timeline

1820(?)
Araminta 'Minty' Ross was born to enslaved parents, Harriet Green and Ben Ross. Even as a young child, she faced punishment through whippings. To keep warm on cold nights, she would sleep near the fire and, at times, put her toes into the smoldering ashes to prevent frostbite.

1832(?)
Now called Harriet Ross, she was seriously injured by a blow to the head, inflicted by a white overseer for refusing to tie up a man who had attempted to flee.

1844
She married John Tubman, a free black man. Unfortunately, he did not share her dream of traveling North to escape slavery.

1849
Harriet escaped. At the first 'safe' house she was put into a wagon, covered with a sack, and driven to her next destination. Later, she met William Still, one of the Underground Railroad's busiest 'station masters'.

1860
She made her last rescue trip. In the ten years, Harriet managed to rescue over 300 people. She had made 19 trips and never lost a passenger on the way.

1851
She went to get her husband, John, but he had remarried and did not want to leave. So she found more runaways (passengers) to rescue.

1850
Harriet became an official 'conductor' of the Underground Rail Road. She knew all the routes to free territory, and she took an oath of silence so the Underground Railroad would be safe.

1861
Civil War broke out. Harriet tended to newly freed people, scouted into Confederate territory as a spy, and nursed wounded soldiers in Virginia by making medicines from plants.

1869
She wed Nelson Davis, and they enjoyed a harmonious 19-year marriage until his passing.

1895
The government (finally) gave her a military pension of $20 per month, equivalent to $500 approx., but refused to acknowledge her work as a spy. Harriet also became a suffragist.

10th March 1913
Harriet died of pneumonia. She gave her home to the Methodist Episcopal Zion Church, for the elderly.

HELLO

Thank you for reading my book!

I loved learning about this extraordinarily brave woman. Adversity could have been Harriet's middle name because she had every sling and arrow of outrageous fortune pointed against her. However, instead of railing at destiny, she chose to 'follow the North Star'.

From camouflaging behind squawking chickens, to strapping a revolver in her boot, she did everything possible to avoid detection when she ran rescue operations to free people from slavery for nearly ten years!

Harriet Tubman worked in the worst possible weathers when patrols were less likely to be out and about. She also worked as a nurse and spy during the Civil War, actively campaigned for Women's Suffrage, and continued to help newly freed people assimilate into society by providing for them despite her limited means. She gave freely - money, resources, time, talents.
A true hero with a heart of gold and a razor-sharp intelligence.

Her story is one worth telling to children, not only because of her amazing bravery, but also because of her wonderful kindness and indomitable spirit which led her to risk everything to help everyone she could.

If humanity produces people such as this,
there is hope for us, don't you agree?

Ramya

FREE

Check out
www.ramyajulian.com/picturebooks

Help Harriet get to the 'safe house' belonging to the Underground Railroad

— Cut Line
— Fold Line

A cabin of the type often used as a 'safe house' by the Underground Railroad.

wonderful world
Book series

About the Author

Author, illustrator, and dentist, **Ramya Julian** finished her first novel at the age of ten and she avers it was very well received though it was read only by her brother.

She has all the hobbies of a maiden Victorian aunt – reading, writing, painting, crocheting, knitting and sewing, and the temperament of one. When she's not guilt-tripping her two daughters into good behaviour, she can be found devouring books, crafting poems and puns, and chuckling at her own witticisms. She grew up in India and now lives with her husband and their two daughters in London.

She has experienced so much joy through the enchanting artistry of many authors and creators, that she aspires to share at least some of it through her writing.

To see more of her work, visit **www.ramyajulian.com**

www.ramyajulian.com

Also in this series

NEXT IN LINE: MANY MANY MORE WONDERFUL DIVERSE HEROES

TO MY NEWSLETTER
For the latest news and free printables
www.ramyajulian.com

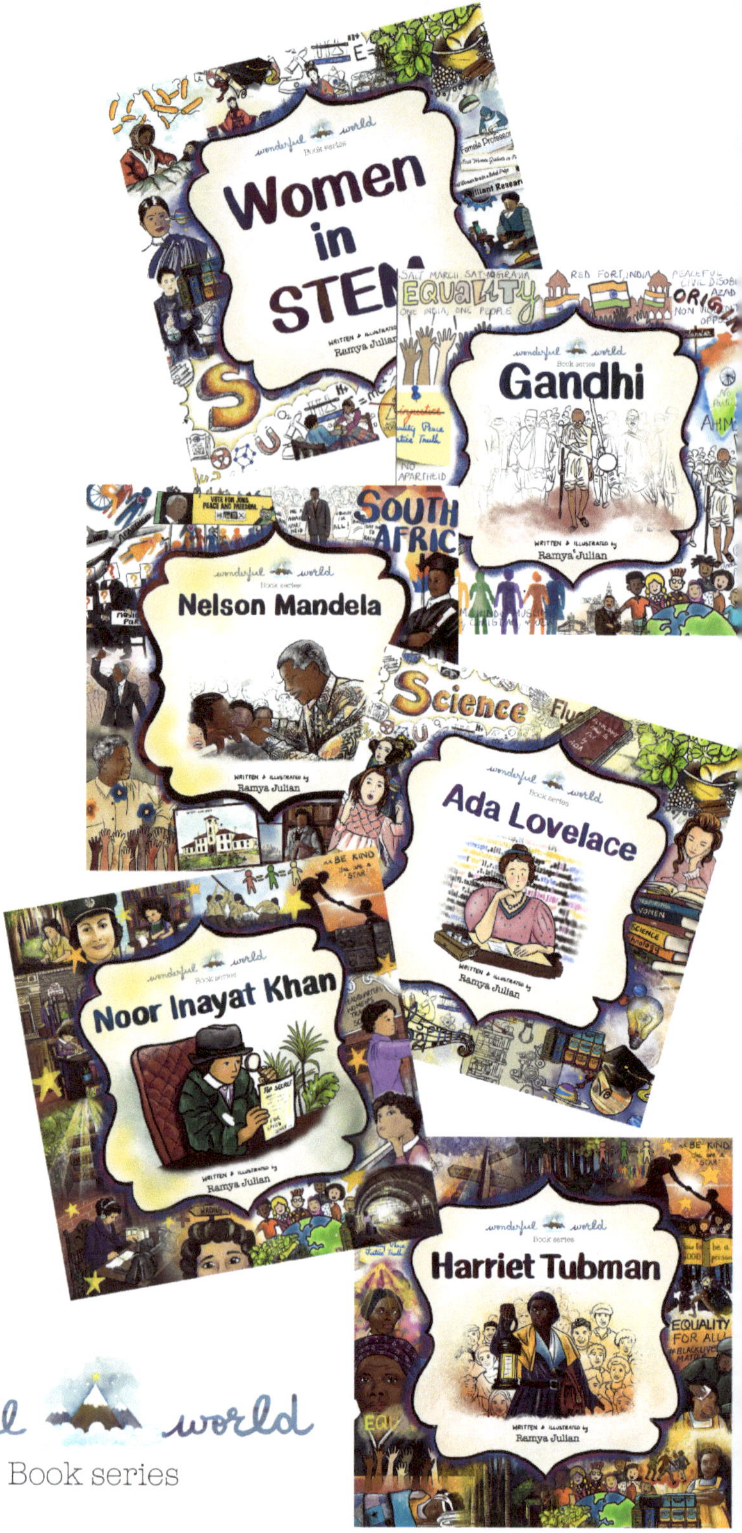

@RAMYAJULIAN

wonderful world
Book series

Journals

FILLED WITH QUOTES FROM FAMOUS CLASSIC NOVELS

Funny Factory Productions™

The perfect gift for book lovers

Available on Amazon

www.ingramcontent.com/pod-product-compliance
Lightning Source LLC
Chambersburg PA
CBHW040022130526
44590CB00036B/57